What a Beautiful Day!

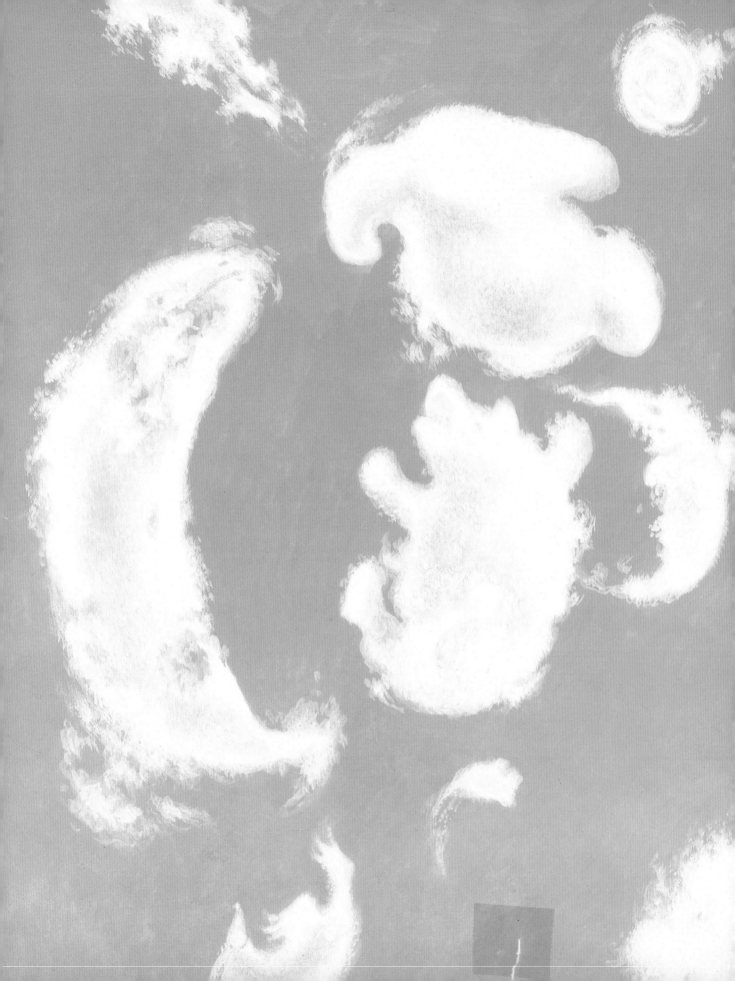

What a Beautiful Day!

by Tilde Michels
illustrations by Thomas Müller

Carolrhoda Books, Inc. / Minneapolis

This edition first published 1992 by Carolrhoda Books, Inc.

Original edition copyright © 1990 by Verlag Heinrich Ellermann,
Munich, under the title WAS FÜR EIN SCHÖNER TAG!

Library of Congress Cataloging-in-Publication Data

Michels, Tilde.
    [Was für ein schöner Tag! English]
    What a beautiful day! / by Tilde Michels ; illustrations by
Thomas Müller.
        p.   cm.
    Translation of: Was für ein schöner Tag!
    Summary: Peter discovers fish, bugs, birds, berries, clouds,
and trees as he spends a summer day in the meadow near his house.
    ISBN 0-87614-739-2 (lib. bdg.)
    [1. Summer—Fiction.] I. Müller, Thomas, ill. II. Title.
PZ7.M5818Wh   1992
[E]—dc 20   91-32987
                                                             CIP
                                                           AC r92

Manufactured in the United States of America

1 2 3 4 5 6 97 96 95 94 93 92

"What a beautiful day!" said Peter as he headed out the back door after breakfast. In one jump, he landed at the bottom of the steps. "I'm going to discover something today." He whistled a tune that he made up as he went along, and he tramped off toward the meadow.

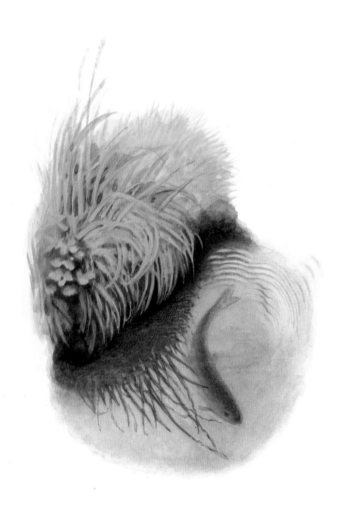

"Hey, fish," Peter said as he came upon the creek and peered over the bank. "I'm off to look for adventure." With a small splash, the silvery fish dived deeper and darted away. Peter hopped over the creek and continued on.

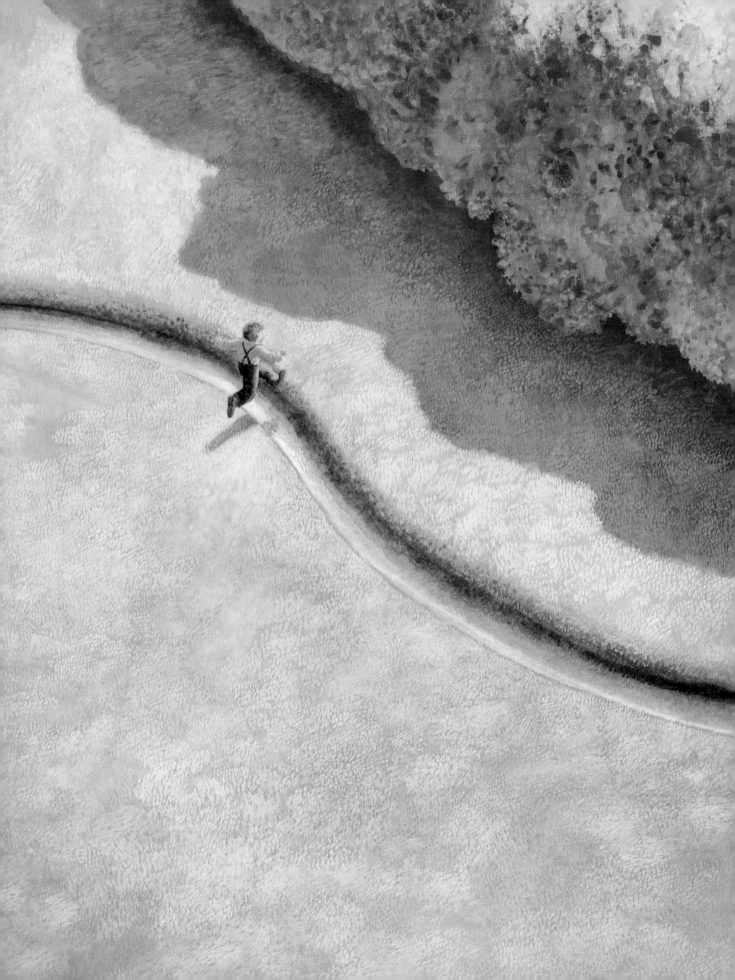

The buzz of dragonflies tickled Peter's ears as he headed through the meadow. He crept up to a dragonfly poised on a leaf. Suddenly, with a flash of wings, the dragonfly buzzed off into the woods.

Maybe that dragonfly was really a fairy, Peter thought. There must be lots of fairies in woods as beautiful as these. He looked for fairies as he made his way along the leafy path. He didn't see any, so he figured they must be hiding or throwing a party.

As he reached the other side of the forest, Peter saw an old hunting stand. When autumn came, hunters would crouch down in it, scanning the land below for deer. But it was summer, so it was safe for Peter to be nearby. Surely he would make great discoveries standing so high above the ground. Very carefully he climbed up to the sunny shelf and squinted into the bright morning sun.

Peter looked out over the treetops at the long stretches of farmland. He watched birds swoop and soar around him. He imagined that he was a bird, flying around the world and discovering new places all the time. But if he were a bird, he wouldn't be able to ride a bike or eat chocolate chip cookies anymore. Being myself has its advantages, Peter thought. Then he saw something that made him doubly glad to be himself.

Below him was a blackberry bush, heavy with ripe berries. Now this is a discovery! Peter thought to himself as he scrambled down from the hunting stand.

Thorns caught and snagged on his shirt when he reached into the bush. But that didn't matter to Peter. He picked some berries and tasted them. They were juicy, sweet, and warm from the sun. After eating several handfuls, he ambled on.

Returning to the meadow, Peter threw himself down
on the grass to rest. A stomach full of blackberries
sure can make a fellow sleepy! The warmth of the
midday sun soaked through his skin and deep into
his bones.

When Peter gazed up at the sky, he saw cloudy
phantoms sailing by. He watched them float together
and then apart. Before the clouds shifted in the breeze,
he found the shapes of a bear and a fish.

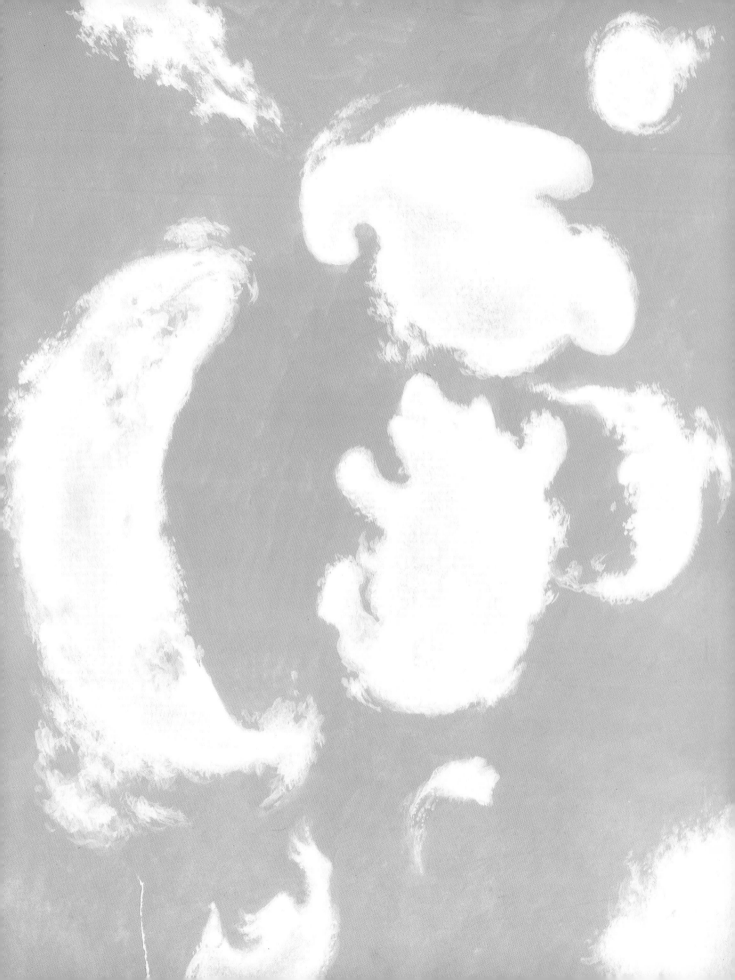

Now Peter was eager to be on his way. He couldn't waste his time resting on such a beautiful day. The land was buzzing with the day's activities as he jumped to his feet. Farm machinery, raising a cloud of dust, growled in the distance. The brush rustled nearby.

Suddenly an owl appeared from the rustling branches. "What are you doing awake in the middle of the day?" Peter called to it. Unanswering, the owl circled above the field before retreating into the forest. A moment later, there was no trace of the owl except a single feather, floating down to rest near Peter's feet.

Passing a large oak tree, Peter paused and looked up. He wished he was big enough to climb among its high, twisted branches. "How old are you, tree?" he asked it. "You're so big I can't even reach around you. You must be a thousand years old!" The branches nodded in reply.

Peter walked by the pasture on his way home. "Look, cow!" he said, showing it the owl's feather. "I made lots of discoveries today. It's too bad you have to stay in the pasture all day. You and I could have fun together." With a stroke of the cow's nose, Peter set off again, this time toward the house. All these adventures had made him very hungry.

About the author

Award-winning author Tilde Michels was born in 1920 in Frankfurt, Germany. Now living in Munich, she is a translator and lecturer as well as an author of children's books. Ms. Michels has published more than thirty-five titles, many of which have been translated for foreign audiences.

About the illustrator

Thomas Müller is a graduate of the Academy of Art in Leipzig, Germany, where he studied art and graphics. Following his graduation in 1979, he worked as a free-lance painter and illustrator. He and his family now live in Göttingen, where he illustrates children's books full time.